W9-BFY-795

PARTNERSHIPS IN URBAN GOVERNANCE

Also by Jon Pierre

BUREAUCRACY IN THE MODERN STATE

CHALLENGES TO LOCAL GOVERNMENT (*editor with Desmond S. King*)

URBAN AND REGIONAL POLICY